CONTENTS

KU-242-189

WHO WERE THE INCAS?

In about the year AD 1200, a group of people came to live in the Cuzco Valley. This valley is high in the Andes Mountains in South America. These people were the Incas.

By the 1500s, the Incas' **empire**, which they called **Tahuantinsuyu**, stretched for more than 3,200 kilometres (2,000 miles) from north to south along the Pacific coast of South America. The Incas ruled over more than 6 million people. They were strong rulers who made sure the people knew what their rights and duties were.

The Spanish arrived in what is now Peru. They saw the Incan cities, roads, and jewellery. Then in 1532, the Spaniards attacked. They killed the Incan ruler and destroyed his empire.

*This big jar is called an aryballus. It was used for carrying liquids such as corn beer, called **chicha**. Jars like this are found only in the Inca empire. The Incas carried the jars on their backs.*

These are part of the ruins of a big Incan city called Tambo Colorado. It was built from mud bricks. The Incas painted red and white patterns on their buildings.

4

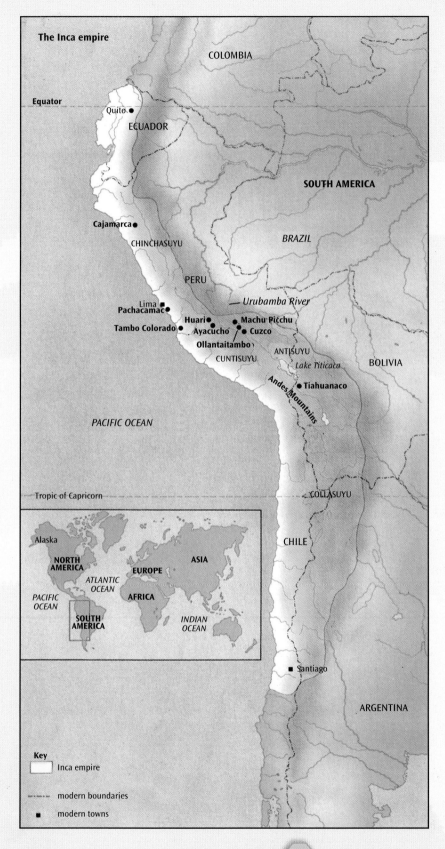

The Inca empire

COLOMBIA

Equator

Quito •

ECUADOR

SOUTH AMERICA

Cajamarca •

CHINCHASUYU

BRAZIL

PERU

Urubamba River

Lima
Pachacamac •

Huari • • Machu Picchu

Tambo Colorado • Ayacucho • Cuzco

Ollantaitambo

CUNTISUYU

ANTISUYU

Lake Titicaca

BOLIVIA

Andes Mountains

• Tiahuanaco

PACIFIC OCEAN

Tropic of Capricorn

COLLASUYU

CHILE

Alaska

NORTH
AMERICA

ASIA

EUROPE

ATLANTIC
OCEAN

AFRICA

PACIFIC
OCEAN

SOUTH
AMERICA

INDIAN
OCEAN

■ Santiago

ARGENTINA

Key

☐ Inca empire

- - - - modern boundaries

■ modern towns

The Incas called their
empire Tahuantinsuyu.
Much of the empire
was on land nearly
3,050 metres (10,000
feet) above sea level.
The empire had huge
snowy mountains and
high plains. The weather
was dry in the summer.
Icy winds blew in the
winter. The Incas grew
crops of corn, grain, and
potatoes. They grew their
crops on hillside **terraces**
in the valleys. They built
canals to **irrigate** their
crops. There was desert
land by the sea. The
people in the desert lived
in **oases** where there
were rivers to water
the dry ground.

HOW DO WE KNOW ABOUT THE INCAS?

We know about the Incas because we can look at evidence from their time that still exists today. We can go to museums to look at tools, cloth, pottery, and gold and silver figurines. We can read what the Spanish wrote in the 1500s about the end of the Inca empire. We can look at what is left of their ruined cities.

Archaeologists are people who are trained to **excavate** and uncover ruins of buildings and cities. They photograph or draw everything they find. They use all this evidence to tell us how the Incas lived.

In 1911, Hiram Bingham, an American, was exploring a dense jungle in Peru. Suddenly, he saw walls and ruined buildings that were half hidden by tangled vines and moss. As the jungle plants were cleared away, a city was uncovered. Hiram Bingham had discovered the Incan city of Machu Picchu.

Sometimes finding out how people lived in the past can help people today. For example, people can rebuild old Incan canals. Then the canals can be used again to water crops. Also, if a crop once grew well for the Incas, then people today could try to grow it again.

Sometimes bumps on hillsides tell archaeologists where Incan sites are buried. The mounds are found by taking photographs from aeroplanes or by walking on trails over the Andes Mountains. These mounds might hide old Incan farms or half-buried religious stones.

Some materials that the Incas used lasted longer than others. Stone houses last for a long time in the mountains. Sun-dried mud walls last for a long time in the dry, hot land by the coast. Pottery also lasts for a long time.

Today, some people in the Andes still keep the old Incan customs. They speak **Quechua**, the Incan language.

*Many people study the Incan sites. Archaeologists, historians, **botanists**, geographers, and other scientists work to tell us more about the Incas.*

CLUES FROM THE PAST

The first people arrived in the Andes Mountains around 12,000 BC. They were **nomads** who lived in caves. They followed and hunted huge herds of animals. Their stone tools are clues that tell how they lived.

By 2000 BC, people had settled down. They grew corn, beans, cotton, and potatoes. They built villages and towns. Some people had special buildings, such as **temples**. Chavin people decorated their stone buildings with carvings. They carved snakes, birds, and big cats into the stone.

About 2,000 years ago, the Mochica people in the north made pots painted with pictures of everyday life. These pictures show that many Incan customs came from this time.

The Mochicas made pots shaped like animals and human faces. They also painted pictures of fishing and weaving on their pots.

BC and AD

Each year has a number. These numbers, or dates, count the years before and after the year Jesus Christ was born. Dates before the birth of Christ have the letters *BC* written after them, for example, 2000 BC. BC stands for "before Christ." Remember that 1000 BC is closer in time to us than 2000 BC. Dates after the birth of Christ have the letters AD written in front of them, for example, AD 900. AD stands for *Anno Domini*. These words mean "in the year of our Lord" in the Latin language.

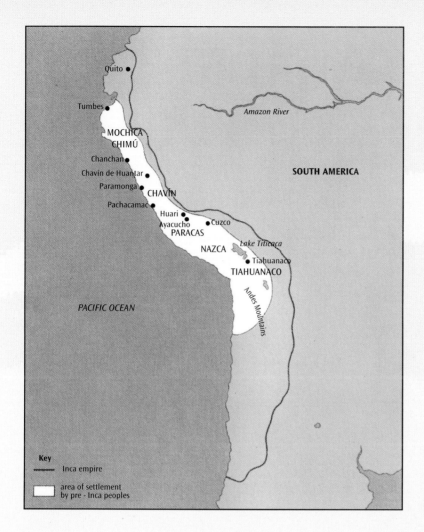

Key
— Inca empire
☐ area of settlement by pre - Inca peoples

The people of Tiahuanaco had a great religious centre near Lake Titicaca. This was long before the Incas. The strong Huari Empire built many roads. They built many towns to control their empire. This empire collapsed around AD 1000. No one knows why. Two hundred years later, the Incas began to build their empire.

The Paracas people wove fine cloth using about 200 different colours. Many of these textiles were made especially to accompany the dead in underground desert cemeteries.

EVIDENCE IN WORDS AND PICTURES

The Incas kept records and passed on information, but they did not have a written language. They told and sang stories, songs, and poems often so they would not be forgotten. They made up story-songs that told of great historical deeds. They used **quipus**. Quipus were long, knotted strings. Each knot stood for a number. Quipus were used to count people, to keep military information, and to keep track of accounts.

Much of what we know about the Incan people comes from letters, reports, and histories written by Spanish soldiers and **priests**. They came to South America to conquer and spread their religion. They usually wrote from the Spanish point of view.

Huaman Poma, a native Indian, is shown in a history written mainly in pictures. Between 1580 and 1620, Poma wrote a book about the Incan people for the king of Spain. The book also shows the Sapa Inca kings in their fine clothing, Incan customs, and the months of the year.

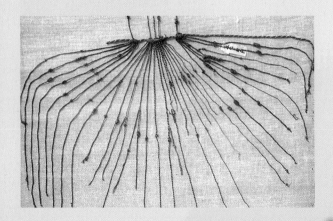

This is a quipu. It has one main cord with coloured cotton or wool threads running from it. It was so exact that everything, even the number of sandals, was recorded.

Some Spaniards said that the Incas were cruel savages. However, the Spaniards never wrote about how cruel they were towards the Incas. Huaman Poma's pictures tell about the suffering of his people.

CÕTADOR·MAIOR·I·TEZORERO
TAVANTIN·SVIO·QVIPOC
CVRACA·CON DOR·CHAVA

Quipucamayocs *were the people who worked with quipus. This drawing by Huaman. Poma shows a quipucamayoc and a counting frame as well as the quipu.*

BUILDING AN EMPIRE

The first Inca ruler was Manco Capac. He founded the Inca capital Cuzco with his brothers and sisters. He said the Sun was his father.

The first eight Incan rulers slowly built a small, strong state. The ninth ruler, Pachacuti Inca Yupanqui, fought a series of battles between 1438 and 1471. First, he won a great victory against the Chanca. Then, he marched against other tribes. Many tribes joined the Incas as allies. They chose not to fight the Incan army. The Inca Empire grew and grew.

*Groups of people called **mitimaes** went to different parts of the Inca empire. They taught the defeated people how to follow Incan customs. They stopped rebellions. They went to the warm southeastern valleys, like the one above, and taught people how to grow tropical crops. Inside the Inca Empire, people had a new, settled way of life and new skills.*

The Inca Dynasty	Year
Manco Capac	about 1200
Sinchi Roca	
Lloque Yupanqui	
Mayta Capac	
Capac Yupanqui	
Inca Roca	
Yahuar Huacac	about 1400
Viracocha Inca	
Pachacuti Inca Yupanqui	1438–1471
Tupa Inca Yupanqui	1471–1493
Huayna Capac	1493–1525
Huascar	1525–1532
Atahuallpa	1532–1533

After this, the Inca rulers had no real power.

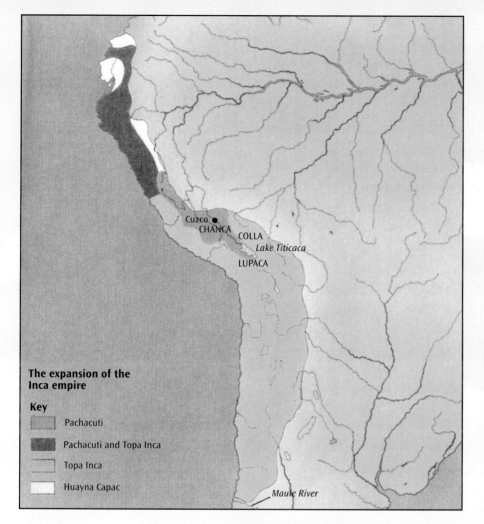

The expansion of the Inca empire

Key

- Pachacuti
- Pachacuti and Topa Inca
- Topa Inca
- Huayna Capac

Cuzco
CHANCA
COLLA
Lake Titicaca
LUPACA
Maule River

The Incan ruler, Pachacuti, conquered the Chanca, the Colla, and the Lupaca tribes. His son, Tupa Inca, won the northern Andes and desert coast. Then Tupa Inca pushed south to the Maule River. Later, Huayna Capac added new lands in the north.

The Incas wanted the defeated tribes to follow the Incan religion, speak the Incan language, and be obedient to Incan laws. But the Incas respected the ways of the tribes they defeated. Often the local chiefs were allowed to stay in power. However, the chiefs' sons had to go to the Incan capital, Cuzco. There they were kept hostage and had to learn Incan ways. In this way, the Incas hoped that all the people in their empire would behave like Incas.

THE SAPA INCA

Viracocha Inca was the eighth Incan ruler. He called himself Sapa Inca, which means "unique Inca". From then on, all Incan rulers called themselves "Sapa Inca". They were also called "Powerful Lord" and "Son of Sun". They believed that they stood for the Sun on Earth and that they were as powerful as gods. Even great chiefs trembled in their presence.

At the Sapa Inca's court, his relatives had important jobs and special rights. The Sapa Inca had servants called the **yanacona** and a bodyguard of **warriors**. Ordinary people were afraid of Sapa Inca and obeyed him without question.

The Inca's sons

The first Incan ruler married his sister, Mama Ocllo, who was said to be the daughter of the Moon. She was his most important wife. Incas called her the **Coya**. Although the Sapa Inca might have many other wives and children, only his sons who had the Coya as their mother could become the next ruler. It was not always the oldest son who became Sapa Inca. Sometimes the best son for the job became the next ruler.

The Sapa Inca sat on a special throne to receive generals, ambassadors, and officials from all corners of his empire.

The Inca name
The word *Inca* is the name for the original Inca tribe and the Inca ruler who was known as the Sapa Inca.

How the Sapa Inca and Coya lived

The Sapa Inca and the Coya lived in grand palaces. The palaces were filled with beautiful wall hangings and gold decorations. They had patios, baths, and temples. Fine trees, sweet-smelling herbs, and beautiful flowers grew in the gardens. Tame birds flew to the Coya when she called them. The gardens also had butterflies made from flattened gold and "fields" of corn made from silver stalks and golden ears.

Each Sapa Inca built a palace in Cuzco and decorated it grandly. His other palaces were places to rest as he travelled through his empire. The eighth Sapa Inca, Viracocha, built this palace surrounded by farm terraces.

GOVERNMENT AND PEOPLE

The Sapa Inca and his family were the most important people in the Inca Empire. The Sapa Inca had a council of four **apus** to help him rule. They were usually his relatives. Each apu was responsible for one quarter of the empire called a **suyu**. Each suyu was divided into provinces. Governors lived in the provincial capitals. Below the governors came the local rulers, or **curacas**. Then came the district headmen, or **camayoc**. The camayoc ruled over a certain number of households and enforced the Incan laws.

Judges, engineers, and quipucamayocs were also important people in ruling the empire.

Incas who paid taxes had to work for up to five years in the army, in the mines, or on town or village projects. This work time was called "mita". Today, some people in the Andes still work together on projects. This is called "minga".

*The clothes of important **nobles** were decorated with the red, gold, green, blue, and yellow feathers of jungle birds. The feathers were sewn into fine cloth. They made bright patterns.*

Laws

Most Incan laws dealt with land, **tribute**, and labour. If people worked hard, they would be fed and clothed. There were harsh punishments for lying, drunkenness, and murder. These punishments could be whipping or even death.

Taxes and tributes

Each province sent food and goods to the capital in Cuzco as a tribute to the Sapa Inca. Most taxpayers were men over 25 years old. They paid their tribute by working on land that belonged to the state. Nobles, officers, curacas, and women did not pay taxes.

The Sapa Inca and his nobles wore big, gold earrings to show how important they were.

17

INCAN CLOTHING

All Incas wore the same type of clothes, but the fabrics, colours, and designs were different. The clothes and headbands that Incas wore showed their place in society and where their home was. Bright colours, patterned borders, and complicated designs showed a person's importance.

Women wore long, sleeveless dresses with a broad, woven sash wound around their waists. They wore long cloaks fastened in front with gold, silver, or bronze pins. Women had long hair parted in the middle. They held their hair back with a headband, or they plaited it. Their necklaces were made of shell or bone.

Men wore short tunics. Their cloaks were long or short and were fastened with a knot at the shoulder. Men wore grander headdresses and jewellery than women. Noblemen wore gold armbands. Sometimes small gold masks were sewn on their sandals and tunics.

Everyone wore sandals. The men made them from **llama** leather, wool, and a fibre from the aloe plant.

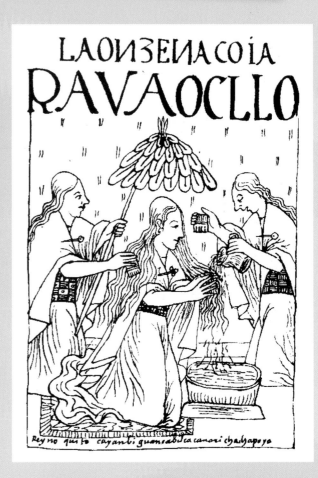

LAONЗENACOIA
RAVAOCLLO

*The Coya and Sapa Inca bathed often. In this picture, the Coya washes and combs her hair, helped by the **nustas,** or royal princesses. The combs were made of long thorns tied to a piece of wood.*

The band of complex designs are known as Tocapu. We do not know what these patterns meant.

Today, women in Otavalo, near Quito, still wear clothes much like those of Incan women.

Royal women wore fancy clothes. They also wore a folded cloth pinned on their hair. The cloth hung down on to their shoulders.

In the mountain areas, clothes were made from fine woollen cloth. They wove the cloth from the fur of animals such as llamas, **alpaca**, or **vicuna**. People who lived in hotter places by the coast wore cotton clothes. More people wore cotton clothes after roads were built and it became easier to trade.

INCAN GODS

The Sun that was called Inti was the most important god in official Incan religion. The Incas believed that they descended from the Sun. Mama Quilla, mother moon, was the Sun's wife. The Sapa Inca represented the Sun on Earth, and the Coya represented the moon.

The Incas believed that the god Viracocha made the Sun, the moon, the stars, the animals, the sea, the earth, and people. Viracocha had three sons that travelled across the land bringing things to life. Viracocha himself travelled down the river until he reached the Pacific Ocean. Then he walked over water disappeared over the western horizon like the Sun.

The Incan gods

Viracocha: the god that brought things to life

Inti: the father Sun of the Incas

Mama Quilla: mother moon, important for working out the months of the year

The stars: children of the Sun and moon. Groups of stars looked after certain things on Earth

Pacha Mama: mother earth, guardian of fertility

Mama Cocha: mother of the lakes and seas

This stone gateway at Tiahuanaco shows a god holding a staff in each hand. It has an elaborate headdress and might represent the Sun, known as Inti.

This is a photograph of the Pleiades, a group of stars. The Incas believed that the Pleiades looked after farming communities and seeds.

The Incas believed that the gods caused earthquakes, floods, storms, drought, and bad luck. They thought that it was important to keep their god happy. They believed happy gods would not let these disasters happen.

When the Incas conquered new areas, they let the conquered people worship their own gods. The gods included the high mountains and local oracles.

Pacha Mama stones, still found today in fields, represented the Incan earth goddess.

TEMPLES AND HOLY PLACES

Inca people believed the gods were all around them. The gods had to be kept happy or disasters would happen. The Incas had holy places, such as mountains and streams, where they made offerings to their gods. These holy places were called **huacas**. There were 328 huacas around the capital city of Cuzco.

Incas worshipped their gods and huacas at special times. Women sowing seeds prayed to Pacha Mama and poured corn beer on the ground. Travellers added a stone to a pile of rocks, called an **apacita**, on a mountain pass to ask for a safe journey. Incas carried lucky charms for protection.

This is Tambo Machay. There were three huacas here. Incas made sacrifices in the main house. They believed the fountain and spring outside were holy places.

Incan miners worshipped the earth goddess, Pacha Mama. They sacrificed llamas so that she would make the earth give up its riches to them. Miners at this mine in Bolivia still sacrifice llamas. Then they have a feast to honour the Pacha Mama.

The Incas built magnificent temples in Cuzco and other cities. Priests looked after these temples. They made sacrifices to the gods, heard people's confessions, and listened to the **oracles**. The head priest, **uillac uma**, was one of the most important people in the empire.

Young women, called **aclla,** served in the temples. Some became **priestesses**. They lived in special houses, called **acllahuasi**, where they wove fine cloth and prepared special food for the gods.

The royal family worshipped in the temples. Ordinary people took part in open-air services in the city centre.

Coricancha, the sun temple in Cuzco, was richly decorated with gold. In the 1600s, the Spaniards built a church on the same site. They used the Inca's stonework.

THE INCAN CALENDAR

Calendars are based on the amount of time it takes for the Earth to go around the Sun. Calendars today divide this time, one year, into 52 seven-day weeks. However, the native indian Huaman Poma, wrote of three ten-day weeks making a month. Incas wrote about an eight-day week.

Incan astronomers, who were usually priests, watched the positions of the Sun, the Moon, and the planet Venus. One historian has studied quipus of Incan astronomers. From these, he decided that the Incas knew exactly how some of the planets moved around the Sun.

The Sun temples at Machu Picchu and Pisac were also astronomical observatories.

One Spanish writer said that the Incas built stone towers on the hills east and west of Cuzco to measure the Sun's movements. These towers no longer exist.

At festivals and feast days, Incas played bamboo flutes and drums. People today still play these instruments. The Incas also had special dances that told about the lives of warriors and farmers. Sometimes they danced to ask the gods for rain or for a victory in battle.

Festivals and ceremonies

The Inca calendar year marked many festivals and ceremonies. Many events had to do with farming.

Inti raimi: June, the feast of the Sun. Great sacrifices, including children, were made to the Sun god.

Chahua huarquiz: July, the ploughing month

Yapaquiz: August, the sowing month. One thousand guinea pigs were sacrificed when the first corn was planted.

Coya raimi: September, the feast of the Coya. Cuzco was believed to be made free of all sickness through special ceremonies.

Uma raimi: October, when people prayed for rain

Ayamarca raimi: November, when the dead were taken from their tombs, paraded around the streets and honoured

Capac raimi: December, special ceremonies when children became adults

Camay quilla: the small ripening in January

Hatun pucuy: the great ripening in February, when guinea pigs and firewood were offered to the Sun in exchange for crops

Pacha Pucuy: the earth ripening in March

Ayrihua: harvesting in April, when a llama was dressed up and taught to eat and drink special food

Aymoray quilla: feasting and dancing at the harvest

MEDICINE AND HEALING

The Incas believed that the gods sent some illnesses as punishments. So, when people were sick, they made sacrifices to the gods. Incas believed other illnesses were caused by magic and so had to be cured by magic.

Every year, during Coya rami, warriors ran from Cuzco to the four corners of the empire. Incas believed this drove sickness and evil from the city.

The Incas knew a lot about herbal medicine. They used the bark of the molle tree for healing wounds, its twigs for keeping their teeth and gums healthy, and its berries as a soothing syrup. They used cinchona bark, which contains **quinine**, to reduce fever.

The Incas chewed leaves from the coca plant to take away tiredness and hunger. People living in the Andes still do this today.

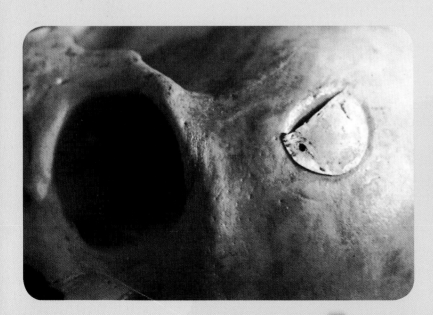

Incan doctors carried out complicated operations. One operation, called trepanning, involved cutting away part of the skull to relieve pressure on the brain. Surgeons then covered the hole with a small, silver plate.

Death and burial

When someone died, his or her relatives dressed in black. Women cut their hair. They held a funeral feast, and everyone danced slowly. Then the body was wrapped in fine cloth and buried. The Incas believed that people lived on after death. The dead were buried with everyday things they would need in their next life. Pottery, baskets, and food were put into the tomb. Warriors were buried with their weapons. Sometimes when a ruler died, his wives and servants were killed and buried with him.

During the Feast of the Dead in November, the wrapped bodies were taken out and paraded in special ceremonies.

Many bodies were buried in tombs made in rocks or caves. On the coast, bodies were buried underground. A dead person's relatives would visit and leave food. Today, people living in the Andes keep the custom of visiting family graves in November.

FAMILY LIFE

Bernabe Cobo was a Spanish priest. From his writings, historians have learned much about the lives of ordinary Incan people.

Boys and girls

Children worked with their families. They learned the skills they would need in adult life. Some girls were chosen to learn how to serve either the Sapa Inca or the Sun god.

Coming of age

When a girl reached a certain age, she fasted for three days. She then washed and dressed in new clothes. At a celebration called the **quicochico** ceremony, she was given her adult name.

Incas wrapped babies tightly and tied them on to a wooden cradle. The cradle was slung on to the mother's back. Mothers in the Andes still carry their babies this way.

When boys turned 14 years old, the Incas held a **huarochico** ceremony. This was always linked to the summer solstice, which occurred in December in the southern hemisphere, and lasted for several weeks. Sons of the Sapa Inca and sons of nobles wore special clothes, ran races, and visited religious shrines. The Sapa Inca gave the boys loincloths and gold earrings. Their discipline, strength, and skills were tested in different ways. At the end, there was a great feast and the boys were given their adult names. Their families gave them weapons and other presents. A more simple ceremony was held for boys in the provinces.

Marriage

Young women married when they were about 20 years old and young men when they were about 25. In Cuzco, the bride and groom were married by the Sapa Inca. In other towns, couples were married by local officials. Later, at home, the bride's father gave her to her husband, who put a sandal on her right foot. Then the families went to the groom's house. The bride gave the groom some special cloth she had woven. Then the feasting and dancing began!

The sons of nobles and government officials went to the house of teaching, the yachahuasi, in Cuzco. They learned about Inca society, government, religion, and engineering. Other children worked with their parents and learned skills from them. Here a modern girl learns about carding wool from an older relative.

LIVING ON THE LAND

In the Inca empire the land was shared between the Sapa Inca, the local chiefs, and the people. Most people were farmers. They worked together in family groups called **ayllus**. The local chief divided up the ayllu land according to each family's needs.

Growing crops

On the high mountain slopes where there were winter frosts, the Incas grew potatoes and kept animals. In the lower, warm, sheltered valleys, they grew corn, fruit, peppers, cocoa, and peanuts. In some parts of the empire, people farmed both high and low land so that they would have a variety of crops. More than 40 different plants were grown before the Spaniards arrived.

The Incas continued to improve their irrigation systems. They diverted mountain streams into new, stone channels, and they straightened rivers.

In some places, the Incas' irrigation systems are still in use. Here a river was turned into a canal so the Incas could grow potatoes.

The Incas built terraces on the hillsides. Terrace walls held back the soil and kept it from being washed away. This increased the amount of flat farm land. Inca engineers planned and built these terraces and the irrigation and drainage systems. The terraces are still in use today.

Taxes from farmers

Married farmers paid their taxes by working on the land of the Sapa Inca and the gods. Then they worked their own fields. When crops were harvested, the Incas kept the harvest in state storehouses. Some produce was sent to Cuzco for the Sapa Inca's family or for the gods.

THE FARMING YEAR

The great Inca festivals followed the seasons and the farming year.

Crops

Ploughing began in August. Everyone worked together, singing praises to the Sapa Inca and the gods. They planted corn and potatoes before the September rains came. In November, Incas irrigated the corn crop. In January, they weeded it. By February, they were digging up the early potatoes and other root crops. The corn ripened in May. Then it was harvested, dried, and stored. The Incas held great festivals and celebrations. The main potato crop was ready in June. At the end of the farming year, the Incas cleared out their channels and prepared the land for the next year's planting.

The Incas used a foot plough to break up the ground. Then women scattered seeds and a curved board was used to scrape soil over the corn seeds.

The Incas used a short hoe with a wide bronze head to dig out weeds. Farmers in the Andes still use the same type of hoe.

Animals

The Incas looked after huge herds of llamas and alpacas that roamed the high grasslands. The herds, like the land, were divided up between the Sapa Inca, the gods, and the people. Families were allowed to have 10 animals. Each family identified its animals with ear tags.

Incas spun fine fleece from alpacas and wove the thread into fine cloth. Llamas gave coarser wool, which was made into sacks and ropes. Llamas also carried loads for the Incas, and their meat was eaten.

Inca shepherds lived with their families in small huts on the cold grasslands. When they rounded up the llamas and alpacas, they kept them in stone-walled pens.

INCAN HOMES

Incas built their homes from stone, mud, or wood. This depended on the location. In the highlands there was lots of natural stone and the Incas built their homes with well-fitted blocks of stone. The Incas also used mud and grass to make plaster walls. They used wooden frames with thatched roofs. On the coast, houses were made of Sun-dried mud bricks called **adobe** and were painted with bright colours. People who lived in or near to forests built houses with wood, cane, and thatch.

This house at Huilloc, in the Andes, is very like an Incan home. Mountain houses were built of stone and had walls about two metres (six feet) high.

Bolivian houses today are made of adobe. The Incas also built houses like this from adobe.

Incan farmers lived in one-room houses. The houses were dark and smoky inside because there were no windows or chimneys. A thick curtain over the doorway kept out cold air.

There was no furniture inside Incan homes. They hung their clothes on stone pegs. They kept food and other belongings in large, wide-necked jars and baskets. Incas sat on the floor to eat. They slept on the floor, wrapped in blankets.

We know about the Inca people and their houses because a Spanish priest, Bernade Cobo, wrote about them in 1653. We can also get clues by studying the way people live in the Andes today.

Adobe bricks, made from mud and straw, are still used in the Andes. The bricks are shaped and left to dry in the Sun.

The Incas stored food and clothing in large jars.

COOKING AND EATING

The Incas ate plenty of corn and potatoes, which they stored and used all year round. They toasted corn, made it into a kind of porridge, and ground it into flour to make into bread and cake. They left potatoes in the open air to dry. These dried potatoes, called **chuno**, would be good to eat for more than a year.

Father Bernabe Cobo wrote that the Incas made a stew called **locro** from potatoes and other vegetables. They thickened it with a grain called **quinoa** and added meat or fish if they had any. Most people did not eat meat very often. Sometimes they roasted guinea pigs. At feast times, they often ate llama. Wealthy people ate all kinds of food. They ate tomatoes, beans, honey, guavas, avocados, deer, and rabbit.

Preparing food

Women did the cooking. There were two or three round holes on top of a cooking stove to hold the cooking pots. Few trees grew on the highlands, and none grew on the grasslands. So dried llama dung was used as fuel. Women sometimes heated the cooking stoves by burning firewood.

Incas used big, round stones to grind corn. Women rocked a curved stone over the corn to grind it into flour. The Spanish brought new crops, such as wheat, with them.

Guinea pigs ran around Inca houses. They grew fat eating scraps. Then the Incas ate them. In most Inca homes, the stove and sleeping areas were at opposite ends. Sometimes the stove was outside in a shed.

Archaeologists have found Inca cooking pots, bone skewers, bronze knives, and wooden spoons. This flat dish has a duck's head handle. It was found at Machu Picchu.

Meals

Incas ate in the morning and late afternoon. If the weather was good, they ate outdoors. The people used pottery bowls and plates. However, wealthy Incas used gold and silver dishes and drinking mugs.

Women served the meals. They also made beer, or chicha, for feasts. At a feast, everyone gathered outside the chief's home to share their food.

SPINNING AND WEAVING

Women spent a lot of time spinning and weaving. They made clothes and blankets for their families. One woman from each household had to weave a piece of cloth for the state every year.

Inca women spun and wove cotton, wool, and the fibres from the aloe plant. Most of the wool came from alpacas. The finest cloth was made from silky vicuna wool. However, vicuna were wild animals. This made it more difficult to get their wool.

Incas dyed cloth different colours. Their dyes came from plants and animals. Greens and browns came from lichens, and red came from the cochineal beetle.

Huaman Poma drew a picture of an Inca woman spinning thread. She fixed a bundle of wool on to a stick with a forked end. Then she made a thread by pulling out some wool and twisting it. Andean people today still spin in this way.

Fancy weaving

The women of the acllahuasi wove the finest cloth, which was called **cumbi**. They made the Sapa Inca's tunics and special cloth that was burned as an offering to the gods. The royal family wore brocades and embroidered fabrics. Sometimes the royal princesses wove these. At other times professional weavers, who were men, wove the cumbi clothing.

Important cloth

The Incas gave fine cloth as presents to local chiefs throughout the empire. They wrapped statues of their gods in beautiful cloth. When people died, they were buried in their best clothes.

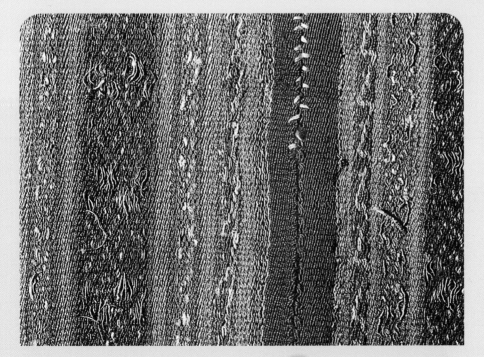

This drawing shows an Inca woman weaving. She is using a backstrap loom. Andean people today weave some of the same patterns on backstrap looms.

The Incas wove gold and silver thread into special cloth.

AN INCAN CITY

Cuzco

Cuzco was the most wonderful city in the Inca empire. It had palaces, temples, and government buildings. The great central plaza was a holy place, **Haucaypata**, where all public ceremonies took place. Four roads led out of the Haucaypata and went to the four regions of the empire. The Sapa Inca and the Coya had their palaces in the Haucaypata. The royal family, nobles, priests, and officials also lived there.

Archaeologists worked in the ruined Incan city of Machu Picchu. They used what they found underneath the ground and the ruins above the ground to help them draw a map of what the city would have been like in Incan times.

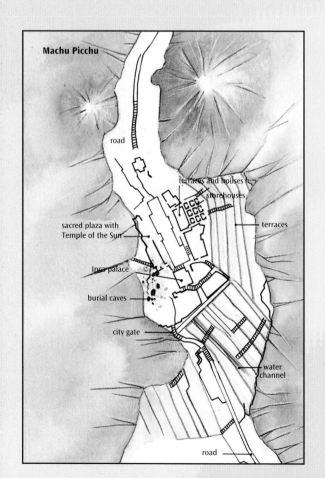

Machu Picchu

road

terraces and houses

storehouses

sacred plaza with Temple of the Sun

terraces

Inca palace

burial caves

city gate

water channel

road

Cities in the provinces

The Incas set up a capital city in each province. Each provincial capital had a governor and staff. They saw that the wishes of the Sapa Inca were carried out in their province. They always lived in the city centre. So did the local rulers, called the curacas. Less important people, like craft workers, lived on the outskirts of the city. Most people lived in small country villages. They only visited the cities on special occasions.

Cities like Cajamarca, Huanuco, Tomebamba, and Quito were important government centres. Machu Picchu was probably a look-out town, guarding an important trade route. Ollantaitambo was mainly a military city.

To get into a city, people went through a tollgate. They had to say why they were visiting the city, and they had to pay a fee, called a toll. This tollgate is at Rumicola, south of Cuzco.

ARCHITECTS AND BUILDERS

Great buildings

Incan buildings had some of the finest stonework ever done. Incan architects first planned their buildings using clay models. Then Incan stonemasons used their great skill to cut and fit blocks together. A huge workforce of thousands of **mita workers** hauled the blocks in place. Incas built temples, palaces, fortresses, terraces, and roads.

Building materials

The most important buildings were made from stone. Sometimes adobe bricks were used to make patterned walls. Near Cuzco, Inca workers dug huge blocks of limestone and granite from the ground.

Inca walls often sloped inwards. This was because the biggest, heaviest blocks of stone were put at the base. Incas sanded and polished the stone blocks. The blocks fitted so perfectly that only a line showed where the blocks joined together.

*Inca doorways and **niches** had stone or wooden beams above them. Doorways narrowed at the top. Incas put stone pegs on the end walls. The pegs were used to tie down the thatched roof.*

Building tools

Stonemasons used hand-held hammer stones to shape each stone. Workers moved the stones with simple tools such as ropes and wooden rollers. Blocks of stone could weigh as much as 18,000 kilograms (18 tonnes). Dirt ramps enabled workers to drag stones to the tops of high buildings and walls.

What remains?

The Spaniards destroyed much of Cuzco. They used the Incas' stones in their own buildings. The Incan walls that are left have survived earthquakes better than modern walls.

This is the Incan fortress of Ollantaitambo. The steep terraces follow the contours of the hillside. Many unfinished building blocks are still at this site.

CRAFTS AND TRADES

Architects, engineers, and craftworkers were important members of Incan society. They did not have to pay tribute. Incan officials made sure these special workers had enough food, clothing, and materials so that they could work full time.

Craft workers made beautiful carvings, high quality pottery, cumbi cloth, and silver and gold objects. These things were not for ordinary people. They were for the royal family, the priests, and the state. Sometimes craft workers were taken from one part of the empire to another. There they taught new workers their skills. However, it is believed that most craft skills were passed on through families.

This tumi knife was made by metalworkers on the coast. It has a gold handle and is decorated with turquoise. Incas may have used it in religious ceremonies.

Incas made drinking mugs, called keros, from pottery or wood. The royal family drank from gold keros.

Metals

Mita workers mined gold, silver, copper, and tin. Incas smelted metal in clay furnaces called **huaria**. The Incas made axe heads, knives, and needles by pouring hot, molten metal into moulds. Gold and silver objects were usually hammered by hand. Very little Incan goldwork remains. Most of it was melted into gold bars by the Spaniards, who then took it away.

Pottery

Incas made coiled pots that they painted with liquid clay. They used bright colours of white, purple, red, and black. They made bold geometric patterns on their pots.

Incas carved figures of small animals and foods such as maize cobs from clay and precious metals. Incan artists used simple tools to make and polish figures such as these stone llamas.

ROADS AND BRIDGES

The Incas built more than 24,000 kilometres (15,000 miles) of roads. Their two main highways ran the whole length of the empire. One highway ran along the coast. The other ran through the highlands. They built stone **causeways** to carry the roads across swampy ground. They built rope suspension bridges to carry them across deep canyons and fast-flowing rivers. Wherever possible, the roads were smooth and paved with stone. The roads helped armies, officials, and goods to travel quickly and easily.

The Spaniard, Cieza de Leon, said that the highway between Quito and Cuzco was the best in the world. The state paid people to keep it clean. There were road markers, storehouses, and lodgings along the way.

Communication

The Sapa Inca needed to know what was happening in his empire. Messengers travelled between Cuzco and provincial capitals. These runners waited for messages and quipus in roadside posts. They relayed them to the next post as quickly as possible. News from anywhere in the empire could reach the Sapa Inca within six days.

Engineers and inspectors planned the highways. Groups of mita workers built the roads.

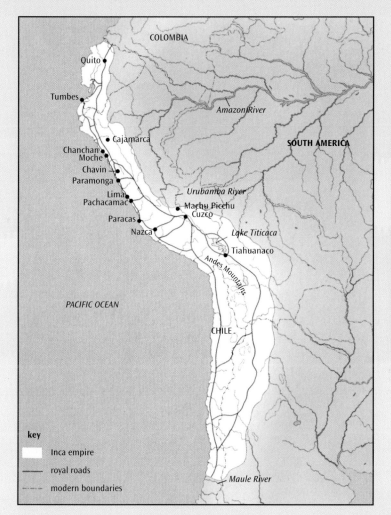

Even in the mountains, Incas built straight, wide roads. Some of the roads had stone safety barriers. Tall posts guided travellers along desert roads. Adobe bricks edged the roads through oases.

Long suspension bridges were anchored to stone towers. Mita workers had to remake rope bridges every year. This modern bridge across the river Ollantaitambo uses Incan foundations.

TRANSPORT AND TRADE

When Incas wanted to go anywhere, they walked. There were no horses or wheels until the Spaniards arrived.

Llamas

Llamas carried loads, but they could not carry more than 50 kilograms (110 pounds). If their load was too heavy, they just sat down. Large herds of llamas took the harvest and tribute goods to Cuzco. However, llamas could only walk about 20 kilometres (12 miles) a day. Incan porters could walk faster!

Money and trade

Incas did not use money. In local markets as well as in the huge Cuzco markets, they simply exchanged goods with each other.

When the Sapa Inca and the Coya travelled, servants carried them in a richly decorated litter, or throne.

Peppers and spices are sold in a modern-day Cuzco market.

48

Incas carried heavy loads on their backs. The load was wrapped in a cloth that was knotted across their chest. Sometimes a rope around their forehead helped support the load.

Mountain Incas swapped wool, potato chuno, and llama meat for the coastal Incas' corn, chilies, fish, and cotton.

Counting

Some Incas used quipus to keep accounts. Other Incas used pebbles or grains of corn to add or subtract. They used scales to weigh gold and silver.

In the mountains, Incas fished in large lakes. They used boats made from reeds like the one in this picture. Along the coast, Incas used wood rafts with cotton sails.

WEAPONS AND WARFARE

The Inca army

The Inca army was well-trained. It was large and it moved fast. Every province sent soldiers with their own banners. Each unit of 10 warriors served under a local leader. These were grouped together in bigger units under a captain who was responsible for 2,500 soldiers. Above him came the commander, who was in charge of 5,000 men. The commander-in-chief was usually one of the Sapa Inca's brothers.

Sacrifices

Before the army set off for a battle, the Incas feasted and made sacrifices. They asked the gods for success.

Soldiers wore quilted tunics and helmets. They had wooden shields. Officers wore richly patterned tunics and plumed helmets.

Incan soldiers fought with slings, spears, bows and arrows, axes, star-headed clubs, blowguns, darts, and stones tied together by cords.

Battles

Incas were good at planning battles. They had more soldiers and better weapons than neighbouring people. They often attacked in places where their enemies least expected.

Incas started a battle by using slings to throw huge stones at the enemy. As the armies got closer, Incas began firing arrows and darts. When the hand-to-hand fighting began, they fought with battle-axes, spears, and star-headed clubs. They defended themselves with wooden shields. All the time, the soldiers shouted and yelled. Others played trumpets, flutes, and tambourines. All of this was to try to terrify the enemy.

Incas built fortresses to protect important towns. The fortresses also sheltered the people of the surrounding area. The Spaniards believed that the huge zig-zagging stones of Sacsahuaman overlooking the city of Cuzco was a fortress.

THE LAST INCAS

Pachacuti (1438–1471)

Pachacuti was the 9th Sapa Inca. The empire grew bigger because of his victory over the Chanca people. He built roads, forts, and cities in his new lands. He made new laws and modernized the army.

Tupa Inca (1471–1493)

Tupa Inca was the 10th Sapa Inca. He made even more conquests and brought more land into the Inca empire. But, under Tupa Inca, the empire grew more difficult to control. There were rebellions and revolts. He sent hundreds of settlers, the Inca mitimaes, into the far corners of the empire. They were supposed to show the people there how to lead an Incan way of life.

The Incas built many fortresses in the northern provinces. These were for the Incan soldiers who were sent by the Sapa Inca to put down rebellions. This fortress is at Ingapirca, where Incan soldiers tried to control the Canari tribes.

This was once an Incan storehouse. It is built on the steep slopes above the Urubamba Valley. Incas stored army supplies, food, and clothing near towns and capitals.

Huayna Capac spent a lot of time in the northern provinces. He built a palace there and improved the roads. He was a fair and just ruler.

Huayna Capac (1493–1525)

Huayna Capac was the 11th Sapa Inca. During his reign, there were earthquakes, tidal waves, and gloomy prophecies. News came of strange, bearded, white men arriving on the coast. Then a terrible illness struck the Incas. It was probably smallpox brought by the Spaniards. Thousands died, including Huayna Capac and his eldest son.

The sons of Huayna Capac – Huascar and his half-brother, Atahuallpa – both wanted to be the next Sapa Inca. There was civil war and Atahuallpa won. However, the Spaniards had arrived.

THE SPANISH CONQUISTADORS

Francisco Pizarro was a Spanish explorer. On his first expedition to South America, he was one of the first Europeans to see the Pacific Ocean. He explored south of what is now Panama and saw a large raft carrying silver, gold, emeralds, and rich cloth. This was his first glimpse of the Inca Empire. Between 1531 and 1532, Pizarro set out to explore the Pacific coast of South America.

In 1532, one of Atahuallpa's messengers visited the Spaniard's camp. He invited Pizarro to visit Cajamarca. Pizarro and about 160 horsemen and foot soldiers set off into the Andes. They marched nervously up canyons to the high passes. They saw huge Inca forts. The Incas could have easily overcome the marching Spaniards.

Inca messengers told Atahuallpa about the white men. One messenger reported that they were brave warriors who rode animals that travelled like the wind. He said that they had sharp swords and threw balls of fire.

The modern city of Cajamarca surrounds the old hilltop site of the Incan town.

In November 1532, Pizarro and his men came out of the mountain passes. They looked down on the farmland of Cajamarca Valley. The tents of an enormous Incan army lay spread out below them.

Diego de Almagro, Hernando de Soto, and Sebastian de Benalcazar were travelling with Pizarro. They were looking for glory and gold. They wanted to expand the Spanish Empire. They wanted to bring Christianity to people they thought were savages.

Atahuallpa was not in Cajamarca. Pizarro sent one of his captains to a nearby bath house to find him. These hot baths can be seen today.

ATAHUALLPA'S WELCOME

Atahuallpa put on richly embroidered clothes and an emerald collar. He was carried on a special throne to the great square in the middle of Cajamarca. He arrived with about 5,000 men. They were going to meet Pizarro.

But earlier that day, Spanish soldiers had hidden themselves around the square. Suddenly, without warning, the Spaniards attacked. They captured the Sapa Inca and killed his nobles. The unarmed Inca soldiers tried to escape, but the Spaniards went on killing until thousands of Incas lay dead.

*Atahuallpa was impressed when he saw the Spanish horses. Horses meant that the **conquistadors** could move quickly through the Inca Empire.*

At Cajamarca, the Spaniards melted down 11 tonnes of gold objects. Hardly any Inca goldwork survived the Spanish conquest. This gold mask is similar to Inca work.

The next day the Spaniards rode into the Inca camp and took all the gold they could find. Atahuallpa offered to fill a room full of gold if he could have his freedom. Pizarro agreed, but he did not keep his promise. After seven months, Pizarro began melting down the treasure he had collected.

The Spaniards accused Atahuallpa of sending for an army to help him. He was sentenced to death and strangled in Cajamarca Square. Now the Incas had no leader. The Spaniards were ready to push on to Cuzco, the heart of the Inca Empire.

The Spaniards crowned Manco Inca, one of Huayna Capac's sons, as Sapa Inca. They thought they could rule through him. But he turned against them and attacked the Spaniards from Ollantaitambo, the fortress shown here. However, Manco Inca did not escape. He was murdered by the Spanish soldiers.

SPANISH RULE

The Spaniards did not pay any attention to Incan customs and traditions. They introduced entirely new ideas, like money, slavery, and the Roman Catholic religion. They also brought new diseases, such as smallpox, measles, and typhus. The Spaniards executed Tupac Amaru, the last Sapa Inca. In the 50 years after the arrival of the Spaniards, the Incan population fell from 6 million to fewer than 2 million. The Inca Empire was shattered.

Spaniards took over lands farmed for the Sapa Inca and the Sun god. They forced people to pay high taxes and to work as slaves in the gold and silver mines. Even Spanish officials wrote in shame about the poverty and hardship that they caused the Incas to suffer.

Today in the Andes, Inca, Christian, and other beliefs are mixed together. The blending of religions sometimes makes it difficult to separate the customs and beliefs.

Llama herds are still kept on the high grasslands. They are still used to carry heavy loads. This one is on the road south of Quito, Ecuador.

This modern statue of Ruminahui is outside the university in Quito, Ecuador. Ruminahui was one of Atahuallpa's great generals. He fought long and hard against the Spanish invaders. Modern Ecuadorians are proud of what he did.

What is left of the Incas?

Many traditions survived the destruction of the Inca empire. At least six million people living today in Peru, Ecuador, and Bolivia speak the Incan language, Quechua. Their food, farming, and houses are much like those of the Incas. They hold village festivals on Incan festival days and make offerings to the huacas.

Evidence of a great civilization lies all around, although there is still a lot to be learned about the Incas.

This is a modern version of an Incan bridge system in which a platform is pulled by ropes.

TIMELINE

BC

12,000   Nomadic people were living in the Andes.

2000   People were farming and making pottery on the Pacific coast of South America.

AD

200–500   The Nazca state flourished on the south coast of Peru.

200–600   The Mochica state flourished on the north coast of Peru.

600–1000   The Huari Empire controlled most of the southern highlands of Peru.

1200   The Incas were established in the Cuzco Valley.

1438   Pachacuti defeated the Chanca tribe and was crowned as the ninth Inca ruler.

1492   Christopher Columbus landed in the West Indies.

1513   The Spaniards reached the Pacific Ocean at Panama.

1522   The Spaniards began to explore the Pacific coast of South America.

1525   The 11th Sapa Inca, Huayna Capac, and his son died from smallpox introduced by the Spanish settlers. Huascar and Atahuallpa fought for the Inca throne.

1532   Francisco Pizarro captured Atahuallpa and killed his nobles and thousands of Incas.

1533   Atahuallpa executed in Cajamarca. Pizarro enters Cuzco. Manco Inca crowned by the Spaniards.

1533–1534 Pedro Sancho de la Hoz and Francisco de Jerez wrote accounts of the first years of the Spanish conquest of the Incas.

1544 Manco Inca murdered.

1553–1554 Pedro Cieza de Leon wrote about the Spanish conquest and many details of Incan life.

1572 The last Sapa Inca, Tupa Amaru is executed by the Spanish in Cuzco.

1580–1620 Felipe Huaman Poma de Ayala wrote his picture history of the Incas and the Spanish conquest.

1653 Father Bernabe Cobo wrote a history of the New World, with detailed accounts of Incan customs.

1911 Hiram Bingham found the lost city of Machu Picchu.

GLOSSARY

aclla girl who served the Inca religion or the Sapa Inca

acllahuasi house for the chosen aclla

adobe sun-dried mud bricks

alpaca animal related to the camel, bred for its long woolly hair

apacita pile of holy stones by a road

apu governor in charge of one region of the Inca empire

archaeologist person who studies what happened in the past by finding and examining old buildings and objects

ayllu organized group of related Incan families

botanist person who studies plants and plant life

camayoc local Incan leader

causeway raised roadway across water

chicha Incan beer

chuno dried potatoes

conquistador Spanish soldier

Coya Incan queen

cumbi fine woven cloth

curaca local Incan chief

empire group of countries or states ruled by one king or queen who may be called an emperor or empress

excavate to carefully dig up buried objects to find out about the past

Haucaypata holy place in Cuzco

huaca place or object of worship

huaria clay oven or furnace with holes in front so wind can fan the charcoal fire

huarochico ceremony in which an Incan boy was given his adult name

irrigate to water crops by channelling water from a river or lake along pipes or ditches

llama small camel-like animal without hump. It was used to carry loads and has woolly hair, which can be spun and woven.

locro Inca stew

mita worker Inca labourer who was forced to do heavy work

mitimaes Incas who settled in different parts of the Inca empire

noble person born into an important family; the group of nobles in one country is called the nobility

nomad member of a tribe that moves from place to place

niche shallow recess in a wall

nusta royal Incan princess

oasis fertile place in a desert that has water and vegetation

oracle place where gods could be contacted; also a person who was able to contact the gods

priest man who carries out all the duties and ceremonies for worshipping the gods

priestess female priest

Quechua Incan language

quicochico ceremony when an Incan girl was given her adult name

quinine chemical found in cinchona bark

quinoa grain used by Incas to thicken stews and soups

quipu strings with knots in them, used by Incas for keeping records

quipucamayoc Inca who worked with quipus

suyu area equal to one quarter of the Inca empire

Tahuantinsuyu Inca empire

temple building or place where people worshipped their gods

terrace area of flat land made on a hillside to increase the amount of farmable land

tribute type of payment paid in goods or work, made to the Sapa Inca

uillac uma chief priest, member of royal family, and important person in the Inca empire

vicuna animal related to the camel, bred for its fine, silky wool

warrior soldier

yanacona servants of the Sapa Inca and the Sun

Further reading

You can find out more about the Incas in books and on the Internet. Use a search engine such as www.yahooligans.com to search for information. A search for the word "Incas" will bring back lots of results, but it may be difficult to find the information you want. Try refining your search to look for some of the people and ideas mentioned in this book, such as "Manco Capac" or "Incan trade."

More books to read

The Incas (Find Out About series), Philip Steele (Southwater, 2001)

Aztec, Inca, & Maya (DK Eyewitness Books), Elizabeth Baquedano (DK Publishing, 2005)

INDEX